Getting through Anxiety with CBT:
A young person's guide

By Dr Ben Gurney-Smith

Series Editor: Dr Claudia Herbert

Contents

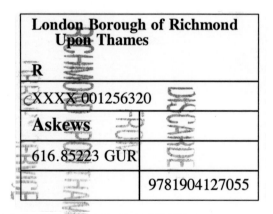

With thanks to Alice Farrington, Claire Holdaway, Louise Dalton, Nicola Connolly and to the young people who made comments on earlier drafts of this booklet. Additional thanks to Dr Jonquil Drinkwater for her comments on earlier drafts.

Introduction

Anxiety is a feeling which is familiar to everybody. Most people, for example, would feel worried before a test or exam. But anxiety can become a problem. We will see how rather than helping people to prepare for something that is worrying, it can make them feel like running away and stop them from enjoying life.

In this booklet we will talk about anxiety and introduce some of the ideas you will be working on with your therapist to get through anxiety using CBT.

What is anxiety?

People describe anxiety in many different ways. Anxiety can be about a fear of a certain situation (called a phobia) or a fear of a number of situations. It can also describe a particular reaction to stress.

Anxiety shows up in our thoughts, feelings, bodily reactions and what we do. It can look like the list below. There may be other things you would add onto the list:

Thoughts
I need to get away
It will be awful
I will show myself up
I will have a heart attack
I can't face it
I won't be able to deal with it
I will lose control
Other thoughts

Feelings
Worried
Nervous
On edge
Scared
Terrified
Other feelings

Body reactions

Heart beating faster
Breathing faster
Sweating
Feeling sick
Butterflies in the stomach
Tense muscles
Jumpy
Wanting to go to the toilet
Other bodily reactions

Things we do (behaviour)

Avoiding places
Biting nails
Not talking to people
Being unable to relax
Pacing
Other behaviour

"No one cares about me"

"I hate myself and my life"

"Things will never get better"

"It's all my fault"

"I'm no good"

"There's no point anymore"

What causes anxiety?

Anxiety can be a reaction to many different things including stress, upset, illness, trauma or worrying things happening to people you are close to. But remember everybody is different. What causes anxiety for one person may not make someone else quite so worried. So why do we get anxious?

A long time ago when we lived in caves, people were surrounded by many dangers such as wild animals. When faced with danger, anxiety helped people by quickly preparing their bodies to react. Just imagine how you might react if you came face to face with a hungry lion! Anxiety sends a message to the body either to freeze, run away or get ready to fight.

If you literally 'froze' on the spot and remained completely still, there might be a chance that the lion might not see you. The lion might then walk the other way and you would not have to waste important energy running off or getting ready to fight. But if the lion spotted you, you would need to run away or prepare yourself to fight to survive. But how does anxiety help our bodies to do these things?

- Anxiety tells us to watch out for danger. This means the body is ready to act if we need it to. This is why people feel 'jumpy' or 'on edge' when they are anxious.

- Legs and arms, important for running and fighting, need blood to work so the heart pumps much faster. This is why people notice their muscles feel tense and their heart speeds up.

- To supply muscles with oxygen in the blood, people breathe more quickly. This can make us feel light headed if we stay frozen to the spot because our body does not use up the oxygen as fast by running or fighting.

- Blood gets moved from other areas of the body which need it less, like the stomach or the head. This is why people feel they have 'butterflies' in their stomach or feel dizzy or light headed.

So without anxiety (a quick reaction to danger) human beings would have become extinct. Nowadays we do not usually have to deal with hungry lions every day! But there are still times when we need our bodies to act quickly, like before a race or if we cross a busy road. Imagine what could happen if you didn't worry a bit about crossing a busy road. So we don't want to get rid of anxiety completely.

When we feel anxious it is important to remember two things:

1) Anxiety does not harm your body *but* it can make you tired if you feel anxious a lot (you are using up energy) and it becomes an uncomfortable feeling (you can feel dizzy, `butterflies', tension in your muscles).

2) Anxiety will disappear by itself in time. The anxiety curve shows us this.

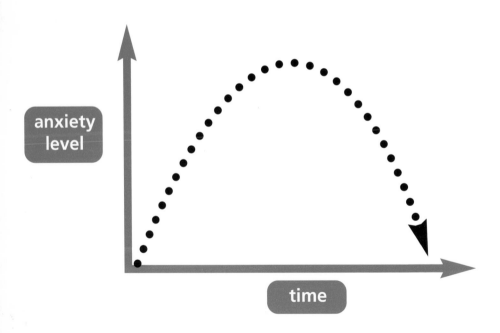

anxiety level

time

The graph shows us that when we are faced with a situation which we think is dangerous, our anxiety goes up and feels uncomfortable. Our body quickly prepares us for danger. When we stay in that situation and are not harmed, the anxiety goes down. This is because our bodies are efficient and designed to save energy.

But when people feel anxiety is a problem they leave the situation when the feelings are uncomfortable; in other words when the anxiety is at the highest point or just before. Although they may quickly feel better, they do not get to find out that they can feel comfortable about that situation.

But how long will it take to feel comfortable? Just as we are all individuals, the time it takes for our anxiety to go down is also different. What we do know is that anxiety will go down in time whoever you are.

To recap what we have learned about anxiety, we know:
- Anxiety prepares the body to react quickly to danger.
- Anxiety can help us to survive in dangerous situations.
- The anxiety curve shows us that anxiety about a situation goes away with time.
- Anxiety can become a problem when we feel unpleasant in a situation and leave before we learn to feel better about it. This can stop us from doing the things we would like to do.

The good news is that CBT will help you get through anxiety so you can enjoy life again. Whatever starts the anxiety, how you think and what you do can keep the anxiety going. CBT tackles anxiety by working on the way you think and do things. The next section explains what this is all about.

Getting through anxiety CBT

CBT is based on the idea that the way we think about things affects how we feel and what we do.

Imagine someone lying in their bed at night and they hear a loud crash downstairs. They might think *'Oh no, a burglar's broken in and is going to do something awful!'* If they thought like that they would feel anxious and worried and would stay awake; perhaps even hide or call the police. But they could think differently. If they thought *'It's that clumsy cat again'*, they would feel differently and be able to turn over and go to sleep (and deal with the mess in the morning!).

In this example, the same thing has happened to the same person but just by **thinking** differently, the same person could **feel** and **do** different things.

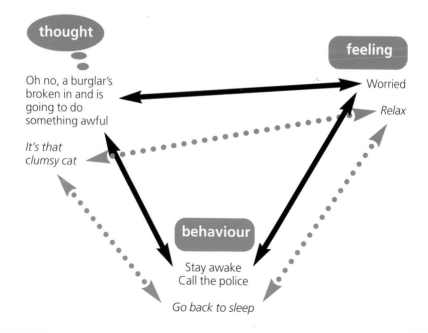

What to expect from CBT

You and your therapist will talk about what is **making** you feel anxious and what is **keeping** you feeling anxious. Your therapist will help you think about how your thoughts, feelings, and behaviour link up. Together, you can draw a map of your problems to help understand them. Together, you will decide what problems to work on. Although your therapist has worked with other people with similar problems remember you are the expert about your life. Getting through anxiety involves:

1. spotting thoughts that make us anxious
2. learning ways to question and change those thoughts
3. learning how to relax our bodies and
4. getting back into situations we would usually avoid

In this guide we will begin with the thoughts, then feelings and then see how you can get back to doing those things you want to do. Just take each step at a time, beginning with the thoughts.

'Sort Your Thoughts'

We will call thoughts which make us feel anxious **spiky thoughts** because they are unhelpful; they 'spike' us by making us feel anxious and uncomfortable. Thoughts that make us feel better we will call '**smooth thoughts**' because they are more helpful; they help deal with situations and relax. When anxiety gets the better of us, spiky thoughts are around. Spiky thoughts that make us anxious make you think that something bad will happen and that you can't deal with it. For example, Levi had an exam and was worried about it. He expected to fail and thought that he could never answer all the questions on the exam paper.

Being able to spot spiky thoughts is the first way to get the better of them. This can be difficult, but if you can begin to spot them, you are well on your way to work out which ones are spiky (and make you feel worse) or those which are smooth (and make you feel better). Let's look at how to catch spiky thoughts and question them to get smooth thoughts and feel better.

Catching spiky thoughts
It will help to 'catch' your thoughts and feelings on a record.

For example:

Situation	Feeling	Spiky Thought
Going to the party	Worried	No-one will talk to me

Thought catching takes a bit of practice. You might have spiky thoughts about how difficult it is to start with. However most people usually find it gets easier with a bit of practice. Noticing a sudden change in how you are feeling can give you a clue that you have had a spiky thought. Here are some questions which you can ask yourself to help catch the spiky thoughts:

- What was going through my mind just before I began to feel anxious?
- What did I think would happen?
- What did I think I could do about it?

With the help of your therapist, you will be encouraged to write down the spiky thoughts as soon as possible before they disappear. Remember there is no escape for spiky thoughts! Once you have learned how to catch them, you will be ready to question them to make them less spiky or smooth.

Looking for evidence

After you have caught the spiky thought, the next step is to question it carefully. You may find there is a different way of looking at the situation which can change the way you feel. To do this, you need to find out what evidence there is to support the spiky thought, and what evidence there is against it. This evidence will help you question your thought – is it really as spiky as you thought it was? It might sound a bit confusing at first, but a bit of practice and following the steps will get you going.

1. Start by writing down all the reasons (evidence for) which you think support the spiky thought.

2. Get together the evidence against the spiky thought being true all of the time. These questions might help you get the hang of this part:

The '**best mate**' question: How would someone else I respect think about this situation? What would they say to make me feel better?

The '**last time**' question: What actually happened the last time I was in this situation?

The '**is it so bad**' question: What if it does happen, what would be so bad about that?

The '**hard time**' question: Am I giving myself a hard time?

The '**time travel**' question: If I travelled in time three years ahead, how would I look at it?

The '**tunnel vision**' question: Am I forgetting what I can do to deal with the situation?

diary can be downloaded from www.oxdev.co.uk

02 / 07 / 2004

Situation	Feeling	Spiky thought	Evidence for	Evidence against	Weighing it all up
Going to the party	Worried	No one will talk to me	Last time I felt really stupid and spent a lot of time on my own	Someone I did know arrived later and I spoke to them.	Maybe there will be people I know going. I managed last time to hang around.

14

3. Weighing it up
   After you have collected all the
   evidence it is time to weigh up the
   evidence for and against the spiky
   thought. Is there another way of looking at the situation
   which does not feel as spiky?

Thinking differently will help you begin to feel less anxious.
Although it can be hard to look at things differently at first, it
gets easier with practice. Gradually it becomes automatic. It is
a bit like learning to swim, you have to think about it carefully
when you're learning, but then you can jump in and swim off.

Testing it out

Sometimes, even though you argue against your spiky
thoughts they can still hang around. The best way to tackle
stubborn spiky thoughts is to test them out for yourself and see
what actually happens. There are three steps to follow:

1. The prediction:
   Place your bets! And write down what you think will
   happen in that situation. This may mean writing down
   exactly what you think will happen, how others will behave
   or what you might do.

get rejected

have fun

get compliments

nothing ch

everyone's

meet new

le

2. The test:

   How can I find out whether this will happen? Find a way to test out whether or not your prediction comes true.

3. The results:

   What actually happened? Did the prediction come true and did anything happen which gave you more evidence about the spiky thought?

Let's look at this in an example:

Dave has been invited to a party. He does not feel like going because his spiky thoughts tell him he will make a fool of himself.

1. Prediction:

   "I will do something stupid, like say the wrong thing and no-one will talk to me".

2. The test:

   Go to the party, approach someone I know when I get there and then ask them how they are.

3. Results:

   "It was really difficult but I said 'Hi' to Nigel and we talked about skating. By the end I was a bit bored actually, as I am not into skating, but my prediction did not come true; I did not say something daft and someone did talk to me (however boring they were!)".

When you have tested it out, you can then use the results to help question the spiky thoughts.

Getting through the feelings of anxiety

Relaxation, like 'sorting your thoughts', is a skill which is meant to be practiced. Relaxation will be something you work on with your therapist to help you feel more confident. Relaxation will help you question your spiky thoughts by helping you remember that there is something that you can do about your anxiety.

There are a number of exercises to help you relax depending on how anxiety most affects you. Together with your therapist you will work out what exercise works best for you. There are three main relaxation exercises which tackle the feelings of anxiety in different ways:

Progressive muscular relaxation

Your therapist may teach you how to control the feelings of anxiety by tensing and releasing important muscles. This is called progressive muscular relaxation. You may be offered a tape to help you learn the exercise and get used to feeling relaxed.

Controlled breathing

You may learn how to relax your breathing. Because anxiety makes your breathing go faster, relaxed breathing helps you bring your breathing under control. By taking slow deep breaths from the bottom of your stomach you begin to control your breaths to feel calmer.

Imaginal relaxation

Using your imagination can also help you leave your spiky thoughts far behind. You might imagine you are somewhere relaxing like an idyllic beach or a place where you have actually been that made you feel happy and calm.

Your therapist will talk to you about all these exercises in more detail. You may be asked to keep a diary to help you decide how well each relaxation exercise is working.

Doing the things you used to avoid

As we know, anxiety will probably have stopped you from doing things you used to do. With your therapist, you will have learned how to get through anxiety by sorting your thoughts and learning how to relax. You may have found yourself in situations you used to avoid when you tested out your spiky thoughts. But it can also help to get through anxiety by taking **small steps** to do the things you still avoid. You and your therapist will decide what situations you will tackle.

Taking things one step at a time can make a scary situation feel much more achievable. This can be helpful if you are worried about one situation in particular, like a phobia. Working out the small steps is called a hierarchy. It is a bit like a ladder where you take steps to get to where you want to go and just like climbing a ladder you will decide when you take the next step.

For example:

Dave was worried about taking the bus to college by himself in case he had a panic attack. With the help of his therapist, they worked out just how worried he was about this by giving the situation an anxiety rating. An anxiety rating is a number from 0 – 10 where 0 means 'no anxiety' through to 10 which means 'extremely anxious'. From there, the therapist and Dave worked on the steps which would allow him to take the bus to college.

Step 1: Riding the bus two stops with a friend   2/10

Step 2: Taking the bus to local shops (three stops)
         home with friend   4/10

Step 3: Taking the bus to local shops (three stops)
         alone   6/10

Step 4: Taking the bus to town with a trusted friend   7/10

Step 5: Taking the bus to town alone (five stops)   8.5/10

Step 6: Taking the bus to college with a trusted friend   9/10

Step 7: Taking the bus to college alone (eight stops)   10/10

Remember the anxiety curve. It is important for the anxiety to begin to disappear so you feel comfortable in that situation before moving onto the next step. You may monitor your anxiety levels in the situation by giving an anxiety rating to ensure you begin to feel comfortable and ready to think about the next step. Sometimes it is possible to move quickly through the steps, at other times you may need to practice some of the steps more than once. In the example above, Dave needed to take the first step a few times before he decided to move onto the next one.

Your therapist might discuss with you tackling one situation you are worried about all in one go. This is called flooding. Flooding can be helpful if it is difficult to break down a situation into small steps. Remember you are the expert about your life and CBT is about working together so you will need to agree what is achievable in one go!

Preparing for the future

Sometimes people find that when things start to get better, they expect them to continue in this way without any hiccups or setbacks. Setbacks can and do happen! You can prepare yourself to deal with these situations by using the skills you have learned. Your therapist will discuss a plan for setbacks before you finish your CBT. Setbacks are an opportunity to test out the skills you have learned. Remember, because they worked before, they will work again. Gradually you will find that the skills you have learned will have you overcome problems more quickly than before.

Finding a therapist

Your General Practitioner (GP) should direct you towards local services where therapy is available free as part of the NHS. There are also organisations that offer CBT on a private basis, in which case therapy would need to be paid for. You have the right to ask about your therapist's qualifications, change therapists if you are unhappy and to check that your therapist is registered with a professional organisation, such as the British Psychological Society (BPS). With CBT, the overall monitoring and accreditation organisation is the British Association of Behavioural and Cognitive Psychotherapies (BABCP). The address for the BABCP is:

BABCP
PO Box 9
Accrington
BB5 OXB

info@babcp.com
Telephone: 01254 875277

Further information

For children in trouble or danger:
`Helping your anxious child: A step by step guide for parents'
By Rapee, R.M., Spence, S.H., Cobham, V. & Wignall, A. (2000) New
Harbinger, Oakland, CA, USA.

www.youngminds.org.uk
An organization for young people, their parents and professionals
concerned about young people's mental health.

www.bullying.co.uk
For people who have been bullied

www.childline.org.uk
For children in trouble or danger
Tel 0800 1111

www.samaritans.org.uk
Samaritans: 08457 909090
jo@samaritans.org

Parents' Information Service
0800 018 2138

Index

Can you help us please?

This is a short questionnaire to help us find out what kind of people read this book, and more importantly, which parts were helpful and which were not so helpful.

Please answer the questions as best you can and return the form to: Blue Stallion Publications, 8a Market Square, Witney, OX28 6BB by post, or complete the online questionnaire at: www.oxdev.co.uk

We assure you that we will deal strictly confidentially with all given information. That means that we would never release any personal information to a third party. We will only use the information to evaluate and improve the books.

How old are you? ☐ years
Are you male or female? Male ☐ Female ☐
Who do you live with? Mum ☐ Dad ☐
   Brothers, how many ☐
   Sisters, how many ☐
   Grandparents ☐
   Other ☐

What made you read the book?

Who recommended this book to you?

Who did you read it with?
By yourself ☐
With a parent(s) ☐
With a doctor/therapist ☐
With someone else ☐

Have you ever been to see a therapist/psychologist to help with your difficulties?   Yes ☐   No ☐

Did the book make therapy any easier for you?

Yes ☐   No ☐

No difference ☐

How helpful have you found this book?
Please mark on the scale below.

1	2	3	4	5
Not at all helpful	Not that helpful	Quite helpful	Very helpful	Extremely Helpful

Did you find it easy to understand?

1	2	3	4	5
Extremely easy to understand	Mostly easy to under-stand	Some easy parts, some difficult to understand	Quite difficult to understand	Very difficult to understand

What was the most helpful thing you learned from this book?

Was there anything you didn't like about the book?

Would you recommend this book to someone else who had difficulties?   Yes ☐   No ☐

Please add anything else that you think might be helpful for us to know.

Thank you for your information!

The Publisher